THIS BOOK HAS BEEN PRESENTED FOR MAKING BETTER WORLD.

WE CAN MAKE BETTER WORLD

I HAVE A STRONG POSITIVE DESIRED TO END POVERTY FROM THE WORLD THAT'S WHY I HAVE STARTED TO WRITE ABOUT ECONOMY MODEL. IF MASS OF PEOPLE CAN UNDERSTAND THE REALITY OF ECONOMICS THEN EVERYBODY CAN COME TO WORK TOGATHER THEN POVERTY WILL BE ENDED WITHIN FEW YEARS FROM THE WORLD. MY IDEAS ARE ON THE BASIS OF HIGHLY REALTY AND INNOVATIVE AS WELL THAT'S WHY I KINDLY REQUEST TO ALL RELATED PEOPLE, PLEASE START TO DISCUSS THIS INNOVATIVE IDEA WHICH MAY BE REALLY USEFUL FOR THE WORLD MAKING BETTER.

I have been badly suffering by poverty in my whole life that's why I cannot enjoy my natural life that's why my intension is that nobody will be compelled to suffer their life like me, who are coming new generation in the world. I kindly request to all readers please read this book by your heart because I am writing by heart to end poverty from the world.

Author - Padam Prasad Chaise, MBS, Tribhuvan University, 2008

Former Finance Manager at JME Remit, Platinum Management College and Vinayak Hospital

Logistic Officer Varun Beverage (Pepsi Company),

Accountant and Internal Auditor for around 20 Organizations.

Currently Cleaner at Turku, Finland since 2016.

Email padamchalises@gmail.com

Mobile No +358469441558

WE CAN MAKE BETTER WORLD

CONTENTS

1. Money

2. Work

3. Productive Work and Unproductive Work

4. International Trade

5. Money Exchange Rate and Money Value

6. Bank and Interest

7. Inflation and Recession

8. Demand and Supply

9. Profit

10. GDP and Growth Rate

11. Tax on Importing

12. VAT, Sales Tax and Profit Tax

13. Property legacy Tax

14. Economy Trapped and Jammed

15. Cost of Labour and Price of All Products

16. Social Benefits

17. Share Market

18. New Economy Model Realism for Developed Country

WE CAN MAKE BETTER WORLD

1. MONEY

In the ancient age, people had been doing transaction by exchanging products. Slowly they had used so many things in different society like special stone, shell, leather, barley, cattle, metal, copper, silver, gold etc. After a few years, they felt hard doing transaction by using those heavy things that's why they created ideas to make small coin on the basis of metal weight. If a person had 1 kg metal then he had been given 1 coin and if a person has 5 kg metal that person had been given 5 coins. All heavy metal had been stored in the centre of society and distributed small coin according to the weight of metal. This idea had been spread in many societies. Slowly society had been ruled by the king. All metal has been transferred under the king house. But after increasing people some people had made duplicate coins. It was believed and fixed ruled that to get those coins, some useful products must be produced and by selling those products and can get those coins. But after making duplicate coins by some people in market useful products had been a shortage and everybody had got a lot of coins.

By knowing this fact, the king had made a plan to stop making a duplicate coin that's why the king had made his picture on the new coin and all old coins had been replaced by new coins with king picture. And the king had said everybody that this was my coins if somebody had made same coins then those people had been given high punishment that's why still people has been given high punishment if people making duplicate money of any country around the world.

After few years' societies were being bigger, only using coins was felt hard to do a transaction that's why they had made printer and one central bank all deposited metal, gold and silver had been transferring to the central bank from king home. And paper money had been printed with king picture and issued on the basis of gold and silver. This kind of system has been continuing now. In reality, all silver and gold are useless metal but they are valued because all society had given value them. To do a transaction everybody can give value for special things. All coins and paper money also just assumed and fake value, those are issued on the basis of the fake and assumed value of silver and gold. That's why all money is well decorated and printed with pictures of a powerful person like a king, emperor, president to attract and to win the people trust.

Now, this assumed money slowly transfer from coin and paper to computer digits. This is good for society, most of the corruption has been possible by using paper money after finishing paper money generation, then corruption will be highly minimized around the world. And all gold and silver also should be made a museum in the front central bank in related countries, coming generation should be known how stupid people had lived in so advance aged. We can easily do international transaction by exchanging digital money with related countries but we still have used gold and silver. This kind of nonsense activities must be known coming generation so the museum must be made in front of the central bank.

Here everybody can get a powerful point that to get money, something valuable products must be produced. If I produce 100 kg maize then I can get money by selling those things. It is the transaction of money using and economic growth. To be clear this point if person A buy my 100kg maize in dollar 50 and he sells it to person B dollar 70 and person B sell to person C dollar 100. In this example, we calculate that our GDP is 100 dollars but in reality, there is nothing increase the real quantity of maize is still 100kg which is really useful for people. But people believed that the economy is being growth by increasing just price of products. 300 years ago, Adam Smith clearly said that a pile of gold and silver is not the wealth of the nation, facilities of people are the real value of the wealth of any nation. Now people are heading to increase the price of products rather than increase real facilities. Most of the economists has read his book but nobody can understand his real pointing points that's why poverty is being existed everywhere. Most the people are busy to increase the price of a product like the above example, but if real products like maize, cloth, home, car, health services etc. increase then people can get more facilities.

WE CAN MAKE BETTER WORLD

2. Work

To increase facilities so many works must be done otherwise, facilities cannot be produced like if we want to eat foods, we must work in the farm, if we want to wear shoes, we must make it. If we want to live in facilities home, we must build it. People have so many desires and want, to fulfil those desires and wants work must be done in related areas. If you want to use a car then your work must be working car manufacturing factory. If your work like cutting grass and throwing river without any purpose then you never get anything. Some people are working in agriculture, some are working making house, some are working foods industries, some are working cloth factories. All those products have been available in the market, people can easily buy a car, who are working in agriculture, people can buy foods who are working in a car factory, it is just an exchange of labour value. We are now also exchanging products with each other as ancient age. In the ancient age, they directly exchange products to products but now we are exchanging products to money and money to products, the main purpose in remain the same. By using money whole economy is being messed up, in ancient age, all people had been working to increase products but the current situation people have been focusing money rather than increasing the necessary products. This is the main problem and drawback of money using in the economy. Money can easily transfer, easily save for future it is the best part of the money but money can be looted, cheated, corrupted, and increased without producing necessary products these are the main drawbacks of money.

People need products, all products are made by using resources and labour. All resources are available in the land. All agricultures have been grown on land, water on land, trees are in the land, stones are in the land, iron is in the land. Whatever resources we need to make useful products those resources are available in the land. By using those resources and labours whatever we need, we can make it. To make any kind of products so many works must be done, if all works are possible to done by using a robot, machine and software then people should not be necessary for working but it is not possible that's why some works must be done by people. To do some works are required special skills, to get those skills people must be trained and educated for a long period and to do some works are not needed special training and education. That's why we should give more facilities who have developed skills and should give fewer facilities who have not special skills. Money is played a vital role to pay worker facilities according to workers skills and working time. So many factories have been producing so many products, those all products have been available in the market, workers have been paid money by the related company according to their work skill and working time period. Those same workers come in the market and buy those same products which they have producing in factories again all money goes to the factory owner. Money just is using as mediator; same people have involved producing products and the same people have used those products. It is a very simple mechanism but people make it unnecessarily complicated by pursing money rather than useful products. Here we can get a very powerful point that people need facilities and products, not a job. If all jobs are possible to be done by AI, then we can use AI. There is not any problem to use AI for anywhere. So many economists have refused to use AI by losing the job of man but they should know clearly that people need products not job.

WE CAN MAKE BETTER WORLD

3. Productive, Supportive and Unproductive Work

In economy, there are three kinds of works one is productive work, which is directly involved in production and distribution function like works of factory, transportation and shopping centre jobs. Second is supportive works, which is involved to support for production and distribution function like bank facilities, insurance facilities, advertisement work and government work. And the third one is unproductive work which is not involved in production and distribution function but that kind of work also should be done like buying and selling of land and home for-profit motive. Land and home must be bought and sold otherwise people cannot buy when they need but most of the people have involved for buying and selling every day to earn a profit, it is the unproductive work of economy. To grow economy something must be produced just assets transfer one person to another to earn a profit, that situation nothing is being grown just increasing the price and getting profit from that kind of transaction is triggering to inflation. If a large number of people have involved that kind of unproductive works, then who have made necessary products. In this situation, obviously, the country is getting lost. For example, in Finland, there are 10 people who are making shoes every day they can make 5 shoes each person, in a month they have made 1500 shoes. Every person can get 150 shoes. In the same time in Nigeria there are also 10 people, there also one person can make 5 shoes per day but in Nigeria, 4 people are involved buying and selling land in the whole month only 6 people have made shoes, after the month they have made 900 shoes. Here each person can get only 90 shoes. By analyzing this simple example, what a big effect in the economy by involving unproductive works. By involving unproductive works, the price will be high in Nigeria. They all have worked in a month but they only get 90 shoes each person but in Finland each person gets 150 shoes means. Price is high in Nigeria; people cannot buy necessary products from the market even they have worked hard. So, the government should make policy to control that kind of unproductive works in the economy.

If all people are involved in really productive areas, then all people can get more facilities and products, if most of the people work in unproductive area then those people can get fewer facilities and products. Another example, 5 people are living in country A those all people are making shirts in one month, they have made 100 shirts of each person. Another country there are also living 5 people, 3 of them are making the same shirt in the month they also make 100 shirts each person. And another 2 persons are buying and selling the same one land each other to get a profit. After 1-month country A has 500 shirts but country B has only 300 shirts because 2 persons of country B has been doing unproductive works. I want to give another example, if government announce that every employee of all company should health checkup in a week and should be holding certificate on the pocket, any time that certificate may be checked by police if employees don't have certificate those employees have been fined of 2 months' salary and all health checkup cost must be paid by a related company. After announcing this decision so many jobs will be created, the tax will be increased but the price of all products is increased because that cost is paid by the company. If the company doesn't increase the price of products then the company goes to bankruptcy. That's why it is necessary to increase all price of products. If the increase in the price of products they people simply cannot buy only a few people can buy more products who have been working with high skills. Look in the economy so many people are doing unproductive works those works easily can be conducted by using AI. In the developed country, all commercial banks can be removed and all money-related work can be handled by the central bank, currently, China has launched it, I have published one book on amazon 3 months ago name I have the dream to end the poverty from the world where I have described about it and I have sent so many countries including China. But I am not sure that they have got the idea from me or not me.

Every day so many lands, houses, assets are selling and buying which can easily be conducting throw mobile app directly buyers and sellers but so many middle agents have engaged to conduct that kind of transaction and getting a commission by that reason price of all necessary products are being expensive and life is being complicated of working-class people. If we look in a small city, so many small shops are open, every small shop has been worked by 2 or 3 people if those 100 shops mix one place by giving equal share like a cooperative model than only around 30 people can be conducting those works which in past around 250 people have been engaged. Those rest of people can be employed in another productive area then all 250 people can get more facilities and products. If this simple idea applies in whole of any country, that country can be super developed country within 10 years if there are some resources. Resources and labours are the main factors of any development, money is just paper, lacking money is not the problem of any country if some resources are available then all kind of developed is possible. So, another powerful point can get that unproductive works finally increase the price of products and decrease facilities of people.

-

-

-

WE CAN MAKE BETTER WORLD

4. International Trade

One person cannot make all necessary products which he has needed that's why products must be exchanged with another person. This same concept also has been applied in the country. One country cannot make all the necessary products that's why every country should involve in international trade. Whatever useful products possible to produce, the country should produce more products and sale to other countries and whatever products cannot be produced inside the country, those products must be bought from other countries. It is the same mechanism of ancient barter system just we have used the money to make easy.

Every country should buy some raw materials and as well as finished products. By involving international trade every country can get benefited. Some products can be made one country cheaply and some products can be made cheaply another country by exchanging those cheap products, all countries can get benefited. If one country is developed rapidly same period other countries also get benefited like currently, China has been rapidly developing, in the same time number of Chinese tourists are being ranked top tourist in many countries around the world. The country should not fight each other for international trade. It should be left free market only some cases should be imposed high importing tax otherwise international trade is being played a vital role to develop any country. other hand China has been developing rapidly means productivity must be increased for rapid development. If productivity is high then all price of products will be cheaper, those cheaper products can be used worldwide that's why all countries can get benefited by developing any country rapidly. So, we can get a powerful point here international trade can get all countries mutual benefited. Some products should be bought from other foreign countries, and some products should be bought by foreign countries. Some foreign citizens come to work inside the country and some citizens go to work in a foreign country. Some tourists come from foreign countries and some tourists go to foreign countries. By that kind of people activities international trade automatically runs on balance.

-

WE CAN MAKE BETTER WORLD

-

5. Money Exchange Rate and Its Value

Every country has its own printed money, this money has been using inside a particular country. If we look in a different country some country has strong money and some country has less valuable money like 1 dollar = Nepalese Rs 122. Why Us dollar is being so strong everybody wants to know, people normally think that US is developed country that's why US dollar is being strong but it is not true because South Korea is more developed than Nepal but South Korea money is very less valuable than Nepal. Every country has its own price level, this price level has been fixing by market from many years ago and gradually increasing. Those countries money is strong, which countries price level is lower. And another hand those countries money is less valuable, which countries price level is high. For example, I can buy 1 kg apple in the US by paying 1 dollar but I should pay for buying same 1 kg apple in Nepal Rs 122 means those country exchange rates are fixed 1 dollar equal to Rs 122.

The money of all countries tie-up with dollar means all central banks of related country exchange rate has been published on the basis of the dollar. So that same time if I exchange one dollar to Directly Nepalese Rs or exchange 1 dollar to Japanese Yen and exchange to Nepalese Rs, I will be got the same amount of Rs. Because if there is possible to get benefit by exchanging money in zero period time then everybody can go to exchange the money then the economy will get the problem that's why all money has been tied up with a dollar. Normally gold, silver US dollar, Euro are accepted by all countries while doing international trade. But very hardly accepted money of developing countries while doing transaction because gold and silver are widely accepted from the beginning of transaction history. The dollar also accepted most of the country because every country can buy anything from any country by paying a dollar. If other countries don't accept dollar then in US market has so many products, any country easily can buy necessary products from US market by paying a dollar, that believing and trusting US dollar is being worldwide accepted money like gold and silver.

Some countries money has been tied up with neighbour country money if there are huge transaction per day like Nepal and India. Indian money has been tied up with dollar but Nepalese money is tied up with fixed-rate like 100 IRS equal to 160 NRS. Between India and Nepal, everyday so many business transactions have been conducted if the everyday money exchange rate fluctuates then many transactions may be badly affected that's why those countries money has been made the fixed exchange rate each other.

By applying a fix exchange rate, the country cannot apply monetary policy effetely while needed. For example, if Nepal needs more foreign currency that easily central bank can devalue own money and then collect more currency but after applying fixed exchange rate Nepalese central bank cannot apply this method this big drawback of the fix exchange rate. And if products are more supply in the market than demand that time also central bank can reduce their own money value then foreign businessman can buy products from there. But in fix exchange rate central bank cannot apply this method. If products are shortage in the market that situation central bank can make strong own money then businessman can buy more products from foreign countries and a shortage would not be existed long period but this mechanism cannot apply in the fixed exchange rate. Another hand if fluctuate rate has been applied then so many people in border areas have involved in money exchange business and hold huge money to get profit which is not good for both countries economy.

Here we should clear that money exchange rate is fixed by the price level of any country and the daily exchange rate is affected by the situation of demand and supply of foreign currency as well as forex market and international trade balance.

WE CAN MAKE BETTER WORLD

6. Bank and Interest

From long years ago all people had deposited their gold and silver in the central bank, and the central bank has been issuing coins and paper money this process is still being continued. To collect money from people and save their money and invest to business to run this kind of money activities, commercial banks had introduced in the economy. Commercial banks have been playing a vital role in money management and to grow economy activities. If commercial banks don't collect money from a large number of people, then it is not possible to create capital for business investment. If we cannot invest in a business then we cannot make the necessary products for people. That's why commercial bank must be running for economic development.

Interest has existed before commercial bank existed. Interest is the gift part of capital lending. How interest was introduced in the economy we can understand by one simple example. One person A farmer cannot cultivate vegetable without money, he must need money for seeds of vegetable and he should work on the land. For this purpose, person A who is firmer can get money from his friend B by requesting for a short period of time supposed he takes money from B Dollar 100 for seeds and he cultivates the vegetables after 5 months, all vegetables are sold in the market and he has earned Dollar 500. By seeing this situation person B said to person A that you have earned more money by using my

100 dollars, if I also use my money same way as you did, today I may have more money like you, so that please give me extra money by adding my original money. Person A has convinced by listening arguments of person B. And person A has paid 100 plus 10 dollars to person B. This extra money is called interest. It is the cost of capital. If interest is high then the price of all products would be high. After introducing commercial banks in the economy, interest practice has been applied rapidly to bear the cost of the bank as well as to earn a profit of the bank. All bank expenses and bank profit are played a vital role to increase the price of all products and services. We can see that inflation is very low where the interest rate is low practice and inflation is very high where interest is high practice.

Money and bank relation crazily function. For example, in Nepal, some of the Nepalese people send a remittance from Finland to Nepal Rs 10000000. 90 % of that money like Rs 9000000, the bank invests to businessman and that money goes to market and again come to deposit at the bank through employees and suppliers who are working and supplying materials to the same businessman. Now they all deposit their money at the bank by Rs 9000000. Again, this money has been invested by the bank keeping 10% for liquidity balance. Now the bank has invested Rs 8100000 to another businessman this process is going to continue. If we look here carefully money is just come in Nepal Rs 10000000 but a bank is able to invest Rs 17100000. So, we can say that really printing money is very less than the actual money in the bank account. Long term investing money is not returned in a short period, if all depositors go to the bank to withdraw money in a short period then the bank will be simply collapsed. This kind of situation may be come in crisis period if the mass number of people feeling that bank is going to collapse then people may go to withdraw their money in a short period but the bank cannot provide them with all money because bank investing money will not be returned in a short period. To control this situation

supports of the central bank must be needed to assure to the people. That's why it is a crazy relation between money and bank.

If bank interest decreases then automatically profit of the bank will be increased. By reducing the interest rate, a lot of new businesses will be operated and production, consumption, employment, demand, supply and tax will be increased. By increasing those factors automatically bank deposit money, as well as investment money, will grow after growing investment automatically profit of bank also increased even interest rate is reduced. Bank work is just money management. By doing this kind of work, the economy never is increased, but without bank work, money management is not possible. At the same time, we should not forget that the high-interest rate is not good for economic growth. If interest is high on loan then the interest of depositors also high but in the bank, very few people have deposited huge amount of money here also get benefited only a few people. Due to interest high price of all products are being expensive that's why working-class people cannot buy products from the market even they have worked hard. This kind of situation will come due to increase in unproductive works and unproductive profit as well. In developed countries, how we can run money handling work without commercial bank I have described it on topic new economy model Realism.

WE CAN MAKE BETTER WORLD

7. Inflation and Recession

Inflation and recession situations are very dangerous for the economy if those situations have happened in the economy then so many people would have been badly suffered and a large number of people would have compelled to suffer by poverty.

Inflation means increasing the price of products and decreasing the purchasing power of money. Short period inflation exists due to increasing by demand and increasing cost of products. In that situation, people should pay more money to buy the same products than normal situation. another hand if the government has given money to poor people as free that kind of money also trigger inflation. Another hand if unproductive works are high in the economy then that situation triggers inflation. For example, if government employees are not used technology that situation number of employees must be high and to pay salaries to a large number of government staff then government must increase the tax on products that's why unproductive works trigger the inflation rate high. this kind of inflation can control by increasing the supply of products. By decreasing unproductive works from the economy. And the cost of production can be reduced by using new technology as well as applying a cost control mechanism. Another way demand can be reduced by tightening credit facilities by the bank. By applying those technique short term inflation can be controlled.

But long-term inflation and hyperinflation have been triggered due to decreasing foreign currency in the central bank. Every country should involve in foreign trade. To do foreign trade every country needs foreign currency at the central bank. If any country exports are decreased and imports are increased then that country foreign currency would be decreased. If foreign currency is decreased that time central bank cannot provide foreign currency as demanding by businessman then central bank compels to devaluate its own money. If domestic money devaluates then price of all importing products will be high. If this situation goes continue few days then obviously hyperinflation situation will come in the economy. For example, a huge amount of oil has been exported by Venezuela and earn a lot of foreign currency, by using that currency, they had imported a lot of products but same time price of oil has been decreased and sales of oil also decreased then obviously their foreign currency has been decreased. After decreasing foreign currency, the central bank of Venezuela must devaluate its own currency otherwise central bank cannot provide foreign currency as demand. If devaluate own currency rapidly then obviously hyperinflation situation would happen. To control this kind of situation, the country must produce necessary products inside the country by using its own resources and should cancel old money and should issue new money to run again. So, hyperinflation situation can be come any time if the foreign currency has been decreased rapidly in the central bank. To prevent this kind of situation, international trade should be near to balance like export and import should not much difference. If Export is greater than import, this situation hyperinflation never is come. But if the import is greater than export regularly long period then hyperinflation may happen any time. Another hand if the import is bigger than export but remittance and tourism is high then hyperinflation would happen even import is greater than export. Finally, it is depended on demand and supply of foreign currency. If the demand for foreign currency is regularly high than its supply that situation hyperinflation will happen.

Recession means the situation of decreasing demand for products and decreasing economy activities as well.

Inflation and recession are a business cycle of the economy but if related persons are continuing more careful about economy activities then they can easily handle before coming any kind of bad economic crisis.

For example, one car manufacture takes a loan from bank dollar 15 billion and another mobile company takes loan 20 billion and one housing company takes loan dollar 50 billion. Those companies have been making their products. To make those products, so many people have been doing jobs in those company and those people have been given salaries by those related companies and those people are going to market and buy products whatever they needed. At the same time if products of those three companies also are coming in the market and being sold continuously in the market then economy activities are being run smoothly. But if those three products of those company are not sold in the market then demand of other products, which are in available in the market, will be highly increased because of demand will be increased due to demand of those employees who are worked in those three companies. That time other company except for those three companies will increase their supply as increasing demand. At the same time if those three products are not sold in the market then those company fired all their employees and stop to produce new products. In this period so many people being jobless, those jobless people cannot buy products then demand will be decreased in market so many products are already supplied but a large number of people being jobless so they cannot buy. If demand is being decreased then the price of other products also decreased and to reduce production as well as production cost so many companies fired their employees again demand will be going to decrease. Another hand those three companies cannot return their loan to the bank, but the bank must pay their customer deposit money if this situation exists long period then this situation called recession and this situation triggering the economic crisis.

To prevent this kind of situation huge loan should not be provided in one area. Another hand if company cannot sale their products in the market then immediately price must be decreased to sale. To decrease price highly, investor-only cannot afford so that to make affordable related bank should remove their interest and government should make tax free for those products after taking those actions, the price will be cheaper and those products will be sold in the market after that those companies may start to make another kind of products by researching market demand. So that if related persons like central bank head, commercial banks head are regularly observing the market situation then that kind of situation easily can prevent before it has come in economy.

-

-

WE CAN MAKE BETTER WORLD

8. Demand and Supply

Demand and supply are the main tools of economics. People have so many necessities, desires and want to fulfil those things, people must work, by working people have produced those things and people have been given money by producer then that money creates the demand and same products come to the market as a supply to fulfil the demand of people. This is the main mechanism of demand and supply. And to create demand people must have money, without money nobody can create demand, nobody wants to sale products as free. That's why to create demand money must be needed. Then how people can get money to create demand, People have been given money by working a job and some people can get money from as taking a loan from friends, relatives and banks. Here also their relatives and friends are getting money by working a job that's why they can give loan to their friends and relatives. Another hand people have deposited their money at bank that money, they have got by working the job, and that deposited money has been given to others as a loan by the bank. That's why money is getting two ways by directly working or taking a loan. People are getting money from profit, interest and commission as well but my focus is here only job and loan. That money can create demand. We have cleared that to get money, somebody must be worked, if works are done in a productive area then something useful products will be produced then same those products are coming to market and same people who are employed to make those products going to buy. It is the simple mechanism of demand and supply.

In the market so many companies have been conducting and running, they have produced so many products, to produce those products, so many people have been working in different jobs. After making products all products are coming in the market and the same people who are working in different companies have been buying products. To run this kind of function so many other sectors have played a role here. For example, banks have been playing a vital role to manage money for conducting this mechanism. And insurance also has been playing a role when an accident gets happened. And advertise agency also has been playing a role to publish advertise and to inform about products to the people. And the government also facilitated so many infrastructures and provided security to run business activities. By taking those supporting activities, an investor should pay interest to the bank, the premium to insurance, commission to the advertising agency, commission to the whole seller, commission to retailers and tax to the government. By paying huge money to those sectors, price of all products will be high, that's why working-class employees who have been really doing hard worked to make those products, they simply cannot buy necessary products from the market. For example, one labour has been working to make a home around 40 years but he cannot buy a home for himself in so many countries like Nepal has the same situation. if increase cost of those above-mentioned supportive activities of a business, the price of all products will be high then people cannot create more demand. If demand is decreased, then obviously supply will be decreased, if supply decreased then so many jobs may be reduced and again demand will be decreased, if that situation is going to long period then economy crisis possible to happen in the economy.

To prevent this kind of situation, a related person like the government should make a rule to reduce the cost of unproductive works as well as removed those unproductive works from the economy by using new technology. Then easily can prevent this kind of situation before it happens. After taking those action price of all products will be cheaper, and people can buy easily, then production, supply, job, the tax will be increased and everybody gets benefited.

In this topic, we should get powerful points that if we produce undemand products in the economy or we unable to sale our products in the market on time then its triggers to the economic crisis. So before making any kind of products, we must analysis demand of those products as well as the income scale of people. For example, if one car manufacture has made expensive cars in Nepal like the price is 1 million Dollar then so many Nepalese have got a job in car factory but that expensive car cannot be bought by Nepalese people, in this situation who have got a job at a car factory, they have bought more others products after that demand of other products would be high then price will be increased and rest of people who don't have worked in car factory they have suffered by inflation. And if a car company cannot sale their products in the foreign market as well then the company may be closed after some period of time. That's why before produce any kind of products, market analysis is the major factors before starting any kind of business.

WE CAN MAKE BETTER WORLD

9. Profit

Profit means sales is greater than the cost. Today I buy one motorbike Dollar 1200 and the same day I sale it on Dollar 1300 means I get profit Dollar 100. If I sale on Dollar 1100 then I get loss Dollar 100. Here bike is remained the same either I get profit or loss just increasing and decreasing the price of the bike can create profit and loss. So, profit is the motivation factor for doing any kind of business. Profit is the gift of the investor by taking a risk on the business. It is not sure that everybody can get profit, sometimes loss may happen it is depended on so many factors.

Profit is also classified into three types, one is productive profit like the profit of productive company, second is supportive profit like the profit of bank and third is unproductive profit like selling of second-hand motorbike.

To motivate investors or innovators, profit must be needed to attract doing business activities but taking maximum profit in a short period, is not good for economic growth. To grow the economy, products must be sold and produced as much as fast. If the investor takes more profit from a short period transaction then the price of all products will be expensive, in this situation working-class people cannot buy more products due to high price of products, so the economy grows is being delayed.

Supportive profit is generated by the supportive business-like profit of bank and insurance. That profit is played a role to increase the price of products that's why that kind of profit is also played a role for delaying to grow economy activities. Profit is needed but getting maximum profit in a short period is trapped the economic growth process.

Unproductive profit is created from an unproductive transaction like selling of second-hand motorbike. The transaction must be conducted to buy or sale of fixed assets but that kind of transactions must be held for necessity, if a large number of people have engaged to conduct this kind of unproductive transaction, then we cannot produce more necessary products in the economy. If we have not enough products, then the price of all necessary products will be high. To grow economy, something new useful value must be added like building a new home then the country can be developed as much as fast. But the increasing price of the old house and getting profit from selling that house is not the real growth of the economy. Profit and tax from this kind of transactions have been played a role to increase inflation.

I want to clear about unproductive profit by example, in the USA and Europe, there are so many casinos have been running under government. The casino also needs for people at occasional so casinos must be conducted in a specific area and must be very few areas. But here the government has been conducting casino everywhere like one small city also we can see 100 casino centres. So many young people have played and lost huge money in the casino every day. And so many staff are working at casinos. By conducting casino, nothing is increasing in the economy just a few people get a job in unproductive areas. By losing money at the casino, people cannot by necessary products from the market. If they cannot buy products from the market then demand, supply, production, jobs and tax would be decreased. If those things are decreased so many people should compel to suffer from poverty. We know the government has used that money which comes casino profit. But due to casino profit, many people should cut their facilities due to losing money, by decreasing economy activities tax of government is being decreased. And another hand those people who are employed at casinos, if those people would have employed in productive areas then economy grow will possible. After that government also can collect more tax from productive areas. Social impact of the casino is not also positive. So many young generations, who are future of country builders are being depressed due to being an addiction to the casino. I don't know why the government is still running because the government has been served by so many talented economists. They should know financially and socially also not profitable to run casino everywhere.

For example, there are two countries like one is Bhutan and another in Nepal. Assumed that both country money exchange rate is equal and labour cost also same both countries have cultivated maize and they both grow same quantity of maize like 1 million kg. in Bhutan price of maize is a little bit high so businessman can get profit over there by selling maize. But in Nepal market price is less than Bhutan by competition of Indian maize. In this situation, a Nepalese businessman is getting lost. if we look very carefully maize is necessary for foods. Both countries have equal maize but just market price is being played a role to make profit and loss. In this situation people of Bhutan have paid more money to buy Maize, that's why they must reduce buying to other necessary products. In Nepal, people have paid less money to buy maize than Bhutan, by saving money due to the low price of maize, Nepalese people can more other products than people of Bhutan. In this situation if Nepalese businessman cannot run business getting loss of market price than the government must take action to save his business, because maize is needed and useful products and so many jobs are created by conducting this business and also due to loss businessman, people are buying cheap maize, the mass of people are getting benefited.

So, profit should not be considered as big matter by government, profit is a big matter for the investor but the government should give priority for the necessity of a large number of people. If the government doesn't protect that business then so many jobs will be ended and maize is also not grown, then government must import from India, which is a big loss of country even country has available useless resources and unemployed manpower. The businessman is always heading to maximize profit may be doing any kind of business like productive, supportive and unproductive but the government should make a rule for motivating them to do productive business by doing productive business if getting loss that situation, the government must compensate to businesses then everybody can get benefited like an investor, employee and government as well.

So, we can get a powerful point here that profit is the motivating factor of the investor, the amount of profit is depended on selling price and other factors as well. If customers pay more price on products then the investor can get profit. If customers pay less price then the investor gets the loss. profit and loss are a big matter for the investor but on the government side, it should not be taken big matter if investor getting loss means a large number of people getting the benefit. All businesses may not go loss every time, sometime few businesses may get lost. that's why the government must protect those businesses that are doing productive businesses, which really produce useful products like growing maize.

Again, in India 100 houses are made and sold and getting profit 2-million-dollar profit. And in Nepal same houses are made and cost also same but selling price is a little bit less that's why in Nepal, the investor gets profit only 1 million dollars. In this case, India economy seems like good but in reality, both countries have the same 100 houses, in Inequality has increased more in India than Nepal due to maximum profit. In that who have bought home in India, those people cannot buy more products as can buy people of home buyers of Nepal. So, tax can be collected more from housing company in India but In Nepal, tax can be collected more from other products those people have more money who have bought cheaper house than India. And Investor of India invests their profit to expand the business and getting more profit, which has played a role to increase inequality problem around the world. But in Nepal, an investor should have taken a loan from the bank to reinvest then interest going to the bank means his profit will be decreased than Indian investor and it helps to minimize growing inequality problems as well.

If a company getting loss continually a few years in that situation government should not support to run continuously. It is good to be closed. But by some reasons, one- or two-years getting loss must be supported by the government by making tax free and the related bank also should make interest free then company can easily survive and everybody can get benefited coming future.

-

-

WE CAN MAKE BETTER WORLD

10. GDP, Per Capita Income and Growth Rate

GDP means gross domestic products. The total monetary value of all products and services which are made in the particular year inside the country. So many methods are used to find out the GDP but mostly has been used an expenditure and income method.

In expenditure method, all products and services have been added with a market price which is produced in a particular year and should be added export and should be deducted import then we can get nominal GDP of any particular year in related country.

In the formula, GDP = value of all consumed products and services + private investing + government investing + value of export – the value of an import.

Here we should clear that if private sectors have invested to open a business that is also growing of economy and if the government has invested to make any kind of infrastructure like making the road that is also growing of economy, that's why we must add those expenditures of private sectors and government sectors to calculate GDP. And all exports products are made inside the country that's why exports must be added to calculate GDP. And people have bought so many foreign products and also use by a private company as well as the government that's why import must be deducted to find out GDP.

In the income method, all related income must be added to find out total GDP. For example,

The income of employment	Rs 100
The income of farming	Rs 50
The income of rent	Rs 40
The income of Interest	Rs 50
Depreciation	Rs 30
Sales Tax Income	Rs 20
Profit	Rs 30
Total GDP	Rs 320
Depreciation [minus]	Rs 30
Net DP	Rs 290

Here we should clear that all income must be added which are getting benefited while making product and services. After adding all related income then we can get the total GDP. In this method, if foreign companies which are working inside the country, the profit of those companies must be deducted and foreign people who are working inside the country income of those also should be deducted. Another hand domestic companies which are operated in foreign countries, and profit of those companies must be added and people of the domestic country, who are working in foreign countries, the income of those people, must be added. Here don't be confused that we have added all income but we also have added depreciation expenses because we are calculating gross domestic products that's why depreciation must be added to calculated gross domestic products. If we don't add depression then our value would be come out Net Domestic Products.

After calculating GDP, Per Capita income can be got out by dividing no of the total population of the country. Those all GDP and Per Capita is the nominal value. By deducting inflation value of nominal GDP then we can get the real value of GDP and Per Capita Income.

PPP GDP means purchasing power parity GDP, it has been addressed the price level of a particular country. for example, nominal GDP has been calculated on the US dollar but the price level of all countries is different so that by addressing price level PPP GDP has been calculated. For example, assumed that Nepal has RS 133000 per capita income and we have exchange rate is 1 dollar equal to Rs 122 then our per capita income is RS 133000/122= 1090 dollar, this is nominal per capita income. To get PPP per capita income, we should find out the price value of both countries like in Nepal around 50 different products prices has been at market Rs 7500 and the total market price of same products in the USA has been dollar 200 then we can find out convert ratio Rs 7500/200 Dollar = 37.5 is the PPP convert rate. Now we can find out by dividing this rate to per capita income Rs 133000. Then we can get 133000/37.5=3547 dollar. Now our nominal per capita income is dollar 1090 and PPP per capita income is 3547 dollars.

GDP growth is calculated on the basis of last year GDP and Current year GDP, for example, assumed that last year GDP was 38 billion dollars of Nepal and this year has been reached 41 billion dollars then we can calculate like this way 41 - 38 =3/38=0.79*100=7.9%. So, here the GDP growth rate is 7.9%.

By calculating GDP, it seems good figure but in reality, there are so many drawbacks of GDP. For example, one cigarette factory has been opened by investing 2 million dollars in India and one hospital has been opened in Nepal by investing the same amount. According to GDP, both countries economy is equal growth but in reality, huge different effects on society by those different investing. Another one, 100 km road is made by using the machine in India by investing 10 billion dollars. But the same kind of road is made only 50 km in Nepal using human manpower and old technology by investing the same amount of money. According to GDP, both countries economic growth is equal but in reality, there is a vast difference length of built road. So big GDP is not indicating economy growth as well as taking facilities of people in a particular country. So, we can get a powerful point here, people need good facilities, not a big GDP and Per capita income. If people are provided with the best facilities by working fewer hours then this is the best indication of best economy situation of any country.

WE CAN MAKE BETTER WORLD

11.   Tax on Importing

Before writing the book named The Wealth of Nation by Adam Smith, all countries believed that huge pile of gold and silver is the indication of a wealthy nation. By that believed all countries have fought in the trade war to increase export and to decrease import. By increasing export, gold and silver would be increased and by increasing importation, gold and silver would be decreased in the country. that's why all countries had imposed high importing tax and had given a high subsidy on exports. By that reason, a large number of people had been suffered from poverty. People were dying by hunger inside the country but leaders were exporting foods to other countries to increase gold and silver. By seeing this situation, Adam Smith had clearly written that having facilities of people is the wealth of any nation. Pilling gold and silver are not the sign of any wealthy nation those things are just metal, we just assumed them to make transaction easy.

After understanding his point, many countries have removed importing tax and subsidy for exporting then all countries started to get mutual benefited. For example, clothes are made in China cheaply than India and foods are made in India cheaply than China that situation China can produce more clothes and India can grow more foods and they can exchange each other on the free competitive market. Both countries can get benefited. So, in normal situation tax on importing should be less rate applied to get benefited. WTO was opened for the same purpose.

But some cases and some conditions applying less importing tax has been a big bad effect on economic growth in a particular country. For example, there are two families in Bangladesh and Nepal. One son of each family has been working in Dubai. Both sons have sent Rs 50000 to their respective family. Assumed that the money exchange rate is equal with both countries. Both families need one wood bed. Father of both families are being jobless and they both know how to make wood bed and wood is also available in the jungle in both countries. In the same time, the same bed can be bought from India which cost is about Rs 45000. To make that bed one person should work 50 days and per day labour cost is Rs 1000. Here Nepalese father thinks that if I make the bed then it takes 50 days and my salary would be Rs 50000. In the same time, I can buy from India Rs 45000, he thinks that it is benefited to buy from India rather than making here. That's why he has bought a bed from India Rs 45000 and bought other products by paying the rest of the money Rs 5000. Father of Bangladesh has made bed himself and has bought so many products from India by paying whole money Rs 50000. Now both countries have one bed but other products have been more in Bangladesh than Nepal. In this case, economic growth is very good in Bangladesh than Nepal. If the father of Nepal has the option to work in another place and may earn Rs 50000 in 50 days then grow of the economy in Nepal also equal to Bangladesh but here situation and condition are different there are no other job options in both countries. In that condition, if Nepal government has imposed importing tax on bed Rs 6000 than father of Nepal can make bed inside the country and get benefited. A same simple example has been happening in Nepal that's why Nepal is being the poorest country in the world.

Maximum resources are available in Nepal and so many jobless people are looking for jobs. And yearly huge amount of remittance has been sent from foreign countries by Nepalese people. But most of the products have been imported from India that's why there is not enough job option inside the country. If some investors invest money in the factory and produce products then those products cannot compete with Indian products inside their own country that's why so many factories and agriculture farm are compelled to close. In that situation applying less importing tax is being a bad effect on economic growth that's why many people are desperately suffered by poverty.

So before making tax policy on importing tax, policymaker should be careful about the impact of economic growth. If products are enough produced inside the country that kind of products should be imposed highly importing tax, it is good to make competition with domestic producers rather than outside competitors if inside productions are enough. In the case of raw material if those raw materials are available inside the country that condition, importing tax must be imposed high rate if those raw materials are not available inside country then it is good to apply free importing tax.

Nepal has imported all fuel from India, due to fuel cost price of all products are being expensive that's why products of Nepal cannot compete with products of India that's why Nepalese investors cannot grow their business inside the country. if the government make free importing tax on fuel then the price of products would be cheaper than current situation after that so many products will be sold from the market, more supply should be increased then so many jobs will be increased and tax will be increased. Government don't get any loss by making the free importing tax on fuel.

So, importing tax is being played a very tricky role, so that policymaker should be very well known while making importing tax. And economists of WTO also should know the effect of importing tax, while making importing tax rule and regulation. Then poor countries should not be suffered by high competition on the global free market.

-
-

WE CAN MAKE BETTER WORLD

12. VAT, Sales Tax and Profit Tax

VAT means value-added tax, VAT is applied in every channel according to increasing its value. For example, assumed that the VAT rate is 10%, the manufacturer has bought raw material Dollar 110 from supplier with including 10% VAT. Here real price of raw material is 100 dollars after processing raw materials manufacturer has made goods and value-added 20 dollars now gross selling price is 100 plus 20 equals to 120 dollars now VAT of 10% of 120 gross selling price is 12 then those 12 dollars should be added on gross selling price to make final selling price now 120 plus 12 equals to 132 dollars is the final selling price for wholesaler. And 12 minus 10 equals to 2 dollars should be paid as VAT to the government by the manufacturer and this process is being gone through every channel. It is a little bit complicated to keep transaction and required extra manpower to keep a record for this purpose. Developing countries where software is not used to keep a record of accounting, then separate staff must be needed to manage VAT related recording, I have seen in Nepal so many accountants are employed for purpose of VAT manage.

Sales tax is very easy than VAT, sales tax is applied only for the final customer. While manufacturer sales to wholesaler and to a retailer that time sales tax is not applied. To calculate sales tax is very simple, there is not required for calculating sales tax to special separate manpower like VAT.

By applying VAT, the government can collect more tax but at the same time price of all products would be expensive, then increasing government tax is not really increasing. So, in my opinion, a sales tax is better than VAT.

Profit is the net income of any business. Normally profit tax is applied on a flat basis like 20 to around 30% according to business areas. Due to the flat tax rate on profit, very few people can gather a maximum wealth of the world so it must be modified by using the new tax system. I have explained in realism model.

WE CAN MAKE BETTER WORLD

13. Property Legacy Tax

It is right to take property from parents if they have wanted to give their property to their children. But due to this kind of property transfer, it is highly possible to increase inequality society on the basis of wealth so to address this kind of problem. Property legacy tax must be applied but there should be condition has been applied. For example, there is only one home, they all have lived together and they don't have other property except that home, in that case, property legacy tax should not be imposed. But if they have a lot of property that time property legacy tax must be applied and the tax rate should be equal to like profit tax on manufacturing company. Because that property is the same as the profit of their children.

WE CAN MAKE BETTER WORLD

-

14. Economy is being Trapped and Jammed

The economic system is a very simple mechanism, from ancient age to now people have deposited gold and silver at the central bank and on the basis those things central bank has been issuing paper money and computer digit money to people. And people have deposited that money in commercial banks. Some people have taken a loan from the bank and produce so many products by employing people. People have been given money as salary by the company. And the company has been sending products in the market, those products have been bought by same people who have been working on production and distribution mechanism by paying same money which is given to them by the company while they have worked in the company. Again, that money is going from market to manufacturer to bank and this process is being continued. This is the real function of the economy. If this process is running continuously and fast, then everybody can get more facilities and country would be developed in a short period. But some reason economy is being jammed and trapped by that reason a large number of people have been suffered to get necessary products even they have worked hard.

If huge money is gone to an unproductive and supportive area like people have employed in a casino that kind of job is an unproductive job, employed a large number of government staff also unproductive area, and a large number of staff at the bank, insurance and advertising agency then price of products would be high. And maximum profit of the bank, insurance, casino, an advertising agency is gone to handful people that's why the price of products would be high for working-class people and they cannot buy products from market by their salary. by that reason, the economy is being trapped and jammed. Another hand salary is the very high scale on top staff compare to working-class people by that reason working-class people cannot buy products from the market even they have worked hard. By that reason, the economy growth process is being trapped and jammed.

-

-

WE CAN MAKE BETTER WORLD

15. Cost of Labour and Price of All Products

All resources are available in the land like sand, water, metal, iron, stone, foods, herbals, trees etc. by using those things to make useable products, labour must be used. All resources are available free of cost. Pricing is started from using labour price. Price of all products are including the cost of labour and profit in the ancient age. But current age also included rent of land, house and interest as well. Those all are also related to labour cost. we can see in USA basic salary is around 1400 Dollars per month that's why all price of products seems less price in the market than Nepal. Basic salary of Nepal is RS 13450 so that the price of all products is the higher price at the market. We can see in South Korea as well there is 8590 Won per hour that's why the price of all products is a high price in the market. So, we can say that price of all products is depended on the price of labour cost. Those market prices are fixed the money exchange rate among the country. That's why the USA dollar is more valuable than Nepalese Rupees and South Korean Won is less valuable than Nepalese Rupees. This mechanism is fixed by labour cost. We have experienced that after increasing the price of labour then instantly increasing the price of all products. That's why by increasing the salary of working-class, they never get benefited because immediately price of all products would be higher.

-

-

WE CAN MAKE BETTER WORLD

16. Unemployment Benefit

If any country has a lot of resources inside the country that country easily can give unemployment benefit to jobless people. We can see in the world so many developed countries have given to their citizen's unemployment benefit but poor countries haven't provided. In my opinion, if resources are available then unemployment benefit can be given to jobless people by any country easily. For example, in Nepal, there are so many resources but banks have faced over liquidity problem, people are facing jobless problem and government are facing a lack of budget to expend running cost as well. In this situation government can decrease interest on agriculture loan as well as home loan then a lot of loans would be issued and start to grow agriculture products and making a home that time so many jobs would be created, so many economic activities would be increased but same time government should have imposed high importing tax on those raw materials and finished products which are available inside the country, and importing tax must be freed on those products which are not available inside the country. After taking those action so many business activities would be increased, and obviously, the tax would be increased those increased tax can be used on social benefit. If the government give unemployment to people, then demand would be increased then the same people can get a job to increase supply. that's why we can say that people of every country, either they should have a job or they should have been provided unemployment benefit, this is the rule of economics mechanism. If both are not given means, there are imposed a wrong economy policy that's why the economy cannot be moved ahead.

-

-

WE CAN MAKE BETTER WORLD

17.   Share Market

To run any kind of business, capital must be invested that's why there are so many ways in practice to invest capital on businesses like a sole proprietorship, partnership business, cooperative model, government business, public-private partnership, a non-profit organization, a foreign company, multinational company and joint-stock company.

Doing business by investing single person and with few partnerships cannot invest huge money on business by that problem joint-stock company had been invented where so many small shares have been issued to the public and can collect huge money to run business. In this system, few powerful persons have seated on the top level and can take the decision to get their benefit. Another hand sole business can be sold on the basis of mutual price understanding with buyers and sellers. By applying the same concept to small share part of the joint-stock company then the whole world is being a big casino. So many people have badly affected by share market price falling. It is a totally wrong concept has been applied by that wrong concept a huge number of people have been wasting time to conduct stock market activities. To grow economy something must be produced which is useful for people but just increasing price is not the reality of economic growth. If one a year there are 100 new homes are built then that is real economic growth, increasing-price of the old house is not an indication of economic growth.

By buying a share, shareholders must be provided dividend if the company have earned profit. But here people dame care about dividend all are involved to increase the price and getting profit. It is only possible on gambling and casino, that's why share market is a big casino, it is not good for society it can be conducted a new way. If shareholders want to sale their sale then those share goes to selling list and somebody wants to buy a share that demand goes to buying list and transactions are made FIFO method in every day and price of a share can be fixed by the related company by calculating total assets minus total liabilities divided by a total number of shares. This price would be published every 3 months by the company then nobody will be suffered share market.

WE CAN MAKE BETTER WORLD

By understanding the above points, we can analyze the current situation.

A large number of people have been suffered by poverty even there are a lot of resources available. Every day a lot of foods have been expired and going to trash and same area people are facing a hunger problem. A large number of people cannot buy survival products even they have been doing hard work. So many companies have been closed due to lack of demand, same time so many people have been suffered to get job and products. Only a few people have gathered a huge wealth of the world by that reason economy grow process is being trapped and jammed. Highly increasing inequality problems around the world, pollution has been highly increased, badly affected climate changed. So, many problems have arisen. People believed that competition market automatically decrease the price of products but unfortunately the huge amount of product cost has been used in advertising by competition that's why huge money is going to advertise agency like google and Facebook after that price of all products are being expensive. All investors have competed on advertising and increasing commission to middle channels to increase sales that's why only a few people get benefited by the free and competitive market.

People need foods, cloths, home, utilities, education, health service, entertainment etc. to get those things, people should not be working so hard as the current situation. People have involved so many unnecessary areas and doing productive works that works have increased all price of above-mentioned people facilities. So, I am going to create a new Economy Model call Realism.

WE CAN MAKE BETTER WORLD

New Economy Model Called Realism

Currently, This Model Only can be Applied in Developed Country like Finland

In realism model, all people must be focused and worked to increased really useful facilities to run their life. People need foods, clothes, home, utilities, car, education, health service, entertainment etc, to get those facilities, if all people work to produce and distribute those things among the society then immediately our working days will be shortened around 15 days per months and working hours also may be decreased.

In this model, all education, health services, security facilities and common infrastructure like building road are conducted by the government and the rest of other economic activities run by people.

Science has invented so many machines, robots and software in the near future most of the works are done by those AI. Then what is the solution? so many people will be jobless those people cannot buy necessary products, then demand, supply and production would be decreased again people must work even AI is available to use, to solve this kind of problem, we must go in realism model. In realism model, people can be freed from work if all works are done by AI.

For example, Finland is the developed country, most people are educated and technology familiar in that situation realism model can be applied.

All small shops can be removed from streets, all commercial banks, insurance, advertisement agencies can be removed, all middle channels agencies can be removed from the economy, they are just doing supportive and unproductive works which have played the role to increase the price of all products. Then we can announce people to invest share on the cooperative. Region-wise one big cooperative can be opened by participating all people of that region. That cooperative can open big shopping centre in so many places according to population, all money related transaction directly can conduct by the central bank through no more paper money is in used. And no more interest has been applying. People have invested share in cooperative that cooperative will make whatever facilities people need. If cooperative need more money that its share capital then central bank directly can provide loan to cooperative without interest. All price of products can be fixed by cost price after that no more any inflation rate will happen. AI can be used as much as possible if jobs are decreased then duty days and duty hours can be decreased among the people. People have rights to holding private property as well as doing their own business. But doing the job in cooperative anyone can be provided with the best quality of life that's why no need to run a single business.

Salaries should not be much difference from top-level to bottom level. To make products, all available resources are used if those resources are available inside the country. Cooperatives will run region wise and buy and the sale can be conducted cooperatively with each other. To manage transportation for people, travel, so many electric cars and bikes are in available in parking as well as the road with free of cost. everybody can use anyone car and bike by using their driving license. Driving license is the key to those cars and bikes. No more VAT is applied only sales tax and Insurance premium has been applied on all selling products. All products are covered by insurance premium while selling products then automatically all property of people and life of people are covered by insurance. While products and services are being sold that time sale tax goes to the government tax office and insurance premium collect by cooperative when accident happen that time that money used to pay related person so that separate insurance business should not be conducted. For example, if one person has made a home that time all products which has used on a home that has paid to insurance premium while buying those products then no more pay yearly. All job wanted people can get a job by dividing related work. All kind of social benefit can be provided by the government. People either get a job or get unemployment benefit.

So many travels, entertainment packaged are conducted inside the countries as well as outside the countries. All products are made according to demand that's why economy never get the problem. All current products are continuing to the sale as market demanding and always focus on new innovative products. Every month the TV show will be broadcast where people can show their innovative ideas and products which is really useful for people. The voting system can be conducted by mobile app. If at least 33% of people accept and vote for new product and then cooperative produce that products and that person, who has created the idea of new products has been gifted by a good amount of prize. After conducting this mechanism, innovation never is ended, more innovative ideas will come than the current situation. After coming new products on sale in the market, all people get notification of mobile app so no more big advertisement which is unproductive work.

All money is handled by digital form by the directly central bank that's why nobody can cheat and corrupt by seating top and decision level. All financial transaction can be seen by all cooperative members on the mobile app. Interest is no more applied, inflation is stopped but other countries inflation is still running that situation by exchange money rate we can manage. After stopping inflation our money is being powerful than other countries every year.

So many cooperatives have not been succussed in our society but that time technology did not support us that's why only a few people were getting benefit by seating top level but the current situation we have a lot of technology by using that technology, our facilities can be increased a lot by working very few hours.

Please start to discuss this model, a large number of people have been suffered by poverty due to lack of knowledge of conducting economic mechanism. This model never gets any problem. Same people work in a cooperative, those people can buy products from the market. People are provided best and quality facilities by working fewer hours than the current situation. not need to operate individual small shops then so many people can be freed from long hours duty.

The single person also can be allowed to do business but profit tax can be applied only around 15% in general but if net profit is more than 10% of its total sales in the year then that profit must be capped by top. At least 15% net profit of its capital in a year, should be allowed to earn.

In Cooperative, profit tax should be applied on 20% on its profit but should be capped from its top because profit goes to a large number of people, due to maximize profit price of all products would be higher for same people that's why they have been provided dividend if profit is more.

People are allowed to buy and sale their property but not allowed middle agents simple transaction would be conducted by mobile app. for example somebody wants to sale their old car then, they put car details and with desire price then directly buyers can buy.

After that people are compelled to do work to increase facilities rather than increasing price, money, and profit. If all people compel to do work to increase facilities then obviously everybody can get more facilities by working fewer hours.

My next book is coming realism model for poor and developing countries.

ONE SIMPLE IDEA CAN BE CHANGED THE WHOLE WORLD. ALL CREATION ARE POSSIBLE BY THINKING DEEPLY ABOUT THE RELATED MATTERS RATHER THAN READING ONLY.

WE CAN MAKE BETTER WORLD

www.ingramcontent.com/pod-product-compliance
Lightning Source LLC
Chambersburg PA
CBHW070849220526
45466CB00005B/1937